Sticker Activity

Numbers

priddy ☺ books
big ideas for little people

1
one

one big car

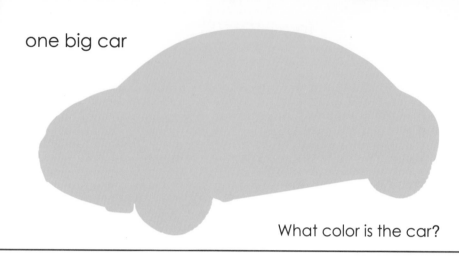

What color is the car?

2
two

two fluffy ducklings

What noise do ducklings make?

3
three

three little babies

Which baby is holding a book?

four juicy red fruits

Which fruit is not
a strawberry?

4
four

five tall
soldiers

Find the soldiers. Are they all the same?

5
five

six little shoes

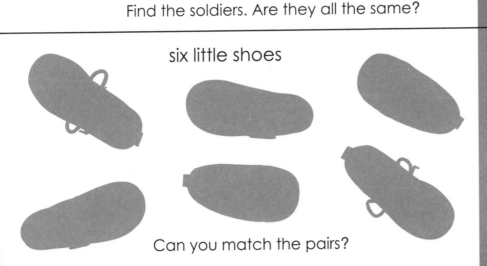

Can you match the pairs?

6
six

7

seven

How many fish can you find?

seven fabulous fish

8

eight

What do we use scissors for?

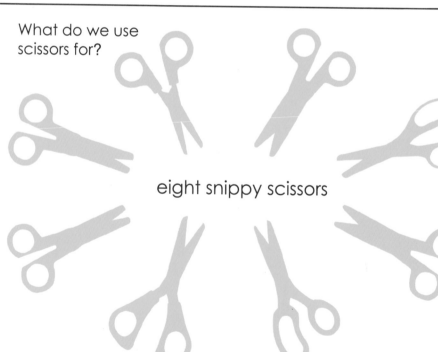

eight snippy scissors

Where do flowers grow?

nine beautiful flowers

9

nine

Which is the biggest star?

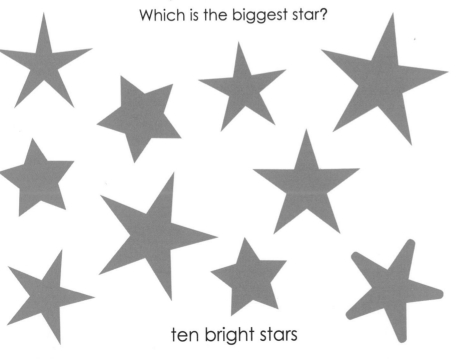

ten bright stars

10

ten

How many leaves?	**5**	five lovely leaves
How many trucks?	**3**	three big trucks
How many pencils?	**9**	nine colored pencils
How many balls?	**4**	four sports balls
How many vegetables?	**7**	seven tasty vegetables
How many hearts?	**6**	six pretty hearts
How many snakes?	**3**	three scaly snakes

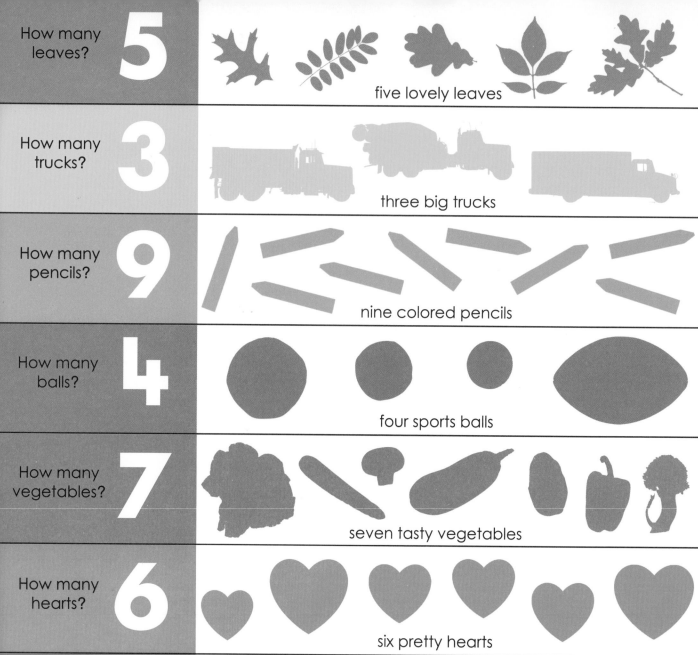

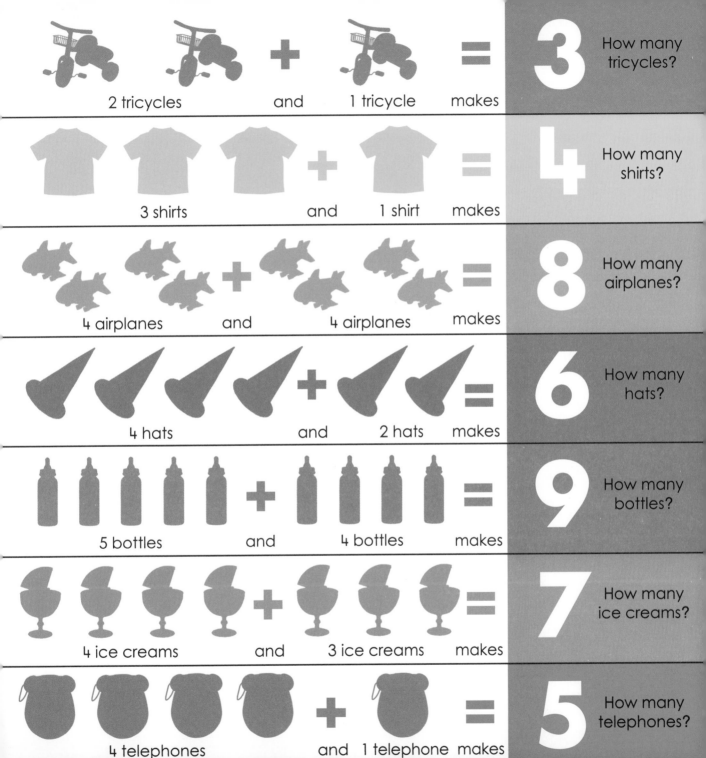

2 tricycles and 1 tricycle makes **3** How many tricycles?

3 shirts and 1 shirt makes **4** How many shirts?

4 airplanes and 4 airplanes makes **8** How many airplanes?

4 hats and 2 hats makes **6** How many hats?

5 bottles and 4 bottles makes **9** How many bottles?

4 ice creams and 3 ice creams makes **7** How many ice creams?

4 telephones and 1 telephone makes **5** How many telephones?

How many clouds?

What is there one of?

Can you count the butterflies?

Are there more goats or pigs?

Can you count the pigs?

How many hens?

How many swans?

What are there two of?

Are there more ducklings or goldfish?

Write in the missing numbers.

1

3

4

6

7

8

10

Can you find where these number stickers belong (there are extras)?

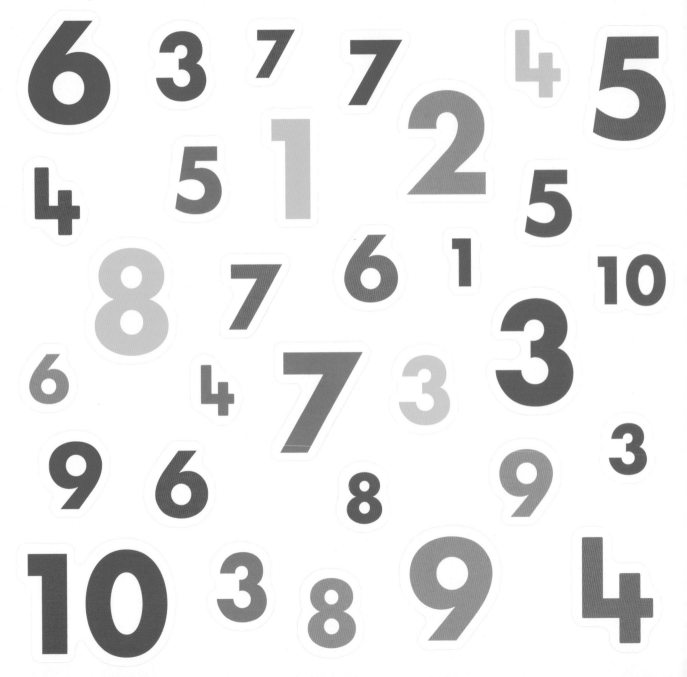

flower

telephone

soldier

fish

pencil

star

goldfish

shirt

heart

shoe

bottle

hat

flower

duckling

goat

pencil

scissors

leaf

tricycle

soldier

airplanes

scissors

pig

duckling

hat

fish

bottle

star

hat

ice cream

raspberry

bottle

soldier

duckling

shirt

star

fish

flower

airplane

heart

goat

telephone

shoe

butterfly

hen

mushroom

bottle

shirt

fish

flower

goldfish

snake

fish

heart

star

strawberry

scissors

pencil

flower

star

baby

flower

ice cream

scissors

broccoli

bottle

butterfly

tricycle

soldier

truck

shoe

hat

heart

leaf

fish

shoe

hen

star

star

airplanes

ball

pencil

duckling

fish

pencil

truck

1 one elephant

2 two shoes

3 three boats

4 four dinosaurs

5

five
pigs

6 six trains

7 seven cupcakes

8 eight airplanes

9 nine ducks

10 ten beach balls

20 twenty flowers

Draw your own picture here.

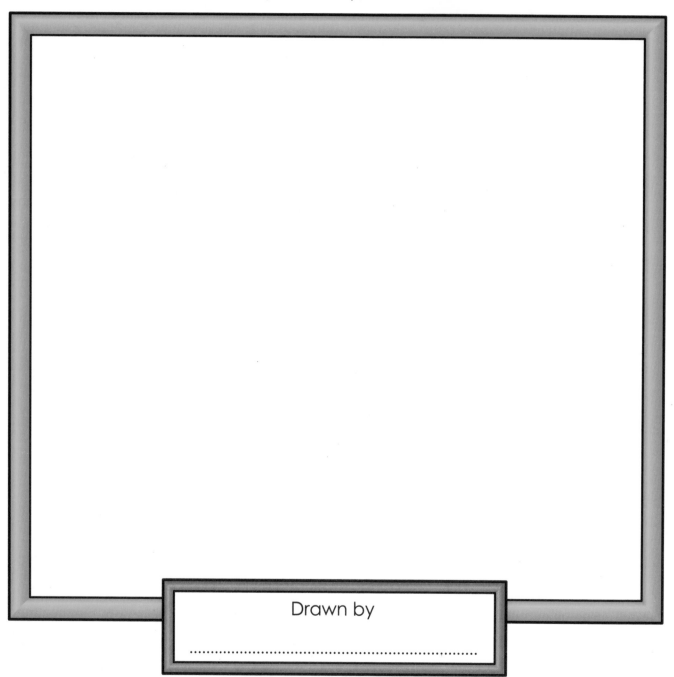

Drawn by

....